SAINT VINCENT DE PAUL

c. 1581-1660

W9-ATK-642

By

F. A. Forbes

"The Spirit of the Lord is upon me. Wherefore he hath anointed me to preach the gospel to the poor, he hath sent me to heal the contrite of heart, to preach deliverance to the captives, and sight to the blind, to set at liberty them that are bruised, to preach the acceptable year of the Lord, and the day of reward."
—Luke 4:18-19

TAN Books
Gastonia, North Carolina

Nihil Obstat: Francis M. Canon Wyndham
             Censor Deputatus

Imprimatur: Edmund Canon Surmont
            Vicar General
            Westminster
            July 2, 1919

Originally published in 1919 by R. & T. Washbourne, Limited, London, as *Life of St. Vincent de Paul* in the series *Standard-bearers of the Faith: A Series of Lives of the Saints for Young and Old.*

ISBN 978-0-89555-621-9

Library of Congress Catalog Card No.: 98-61409

Illustration of St. Vincent taking the place of the Convict (p. 94) by permission of Messrs. Bouasse Lebel.

Cover illustration: St. Vincent de Paul, by Simon Francois de Tours, 1660. Photo: A. Dodin.

Printed and bound in the United States of America.

TAN Books
Gastonia, North Carolina
www.TANBooks.com
2021

SAINT VINCENT DE PAUL

"Blessed is he that understandeth concerning the needy and the poor: the Lord will deliver him in the evil day."

—Psalm 40:2

St. Vincent in the streets of Paris.

"Extend mercy towards others, so that there can be no one in need whom you meet without helping. For what hope is there for us if God should withdraw His mercy from us?"

—St. Vincent de Paul

CONTENTS

CONTENTS

SAINT VINCENT DE PAUL

"Dearly beloved, let us love one another, for charity is of God. And every one that loveth, is born of God, and knoweth God. He that loveth not, knoweth not God: for God is charity."

—1 John 4:7-8

Chapter 1

A PEASANT'S SON

A MONOTONOUS line of sand hills and the sea; a vast barren land stretching away in wave-like undulations as far as eye can reach; marsh and heath and sand, sand and heath and marsh; here and there a stretch of scant coarse grass, a mass of waving reeds, a patch of golden-brown fern—the Landes.

It was through this desolate country in France that a little peasant boy whose name was destined to become famous in the annals of his country led his father's sheep, that they might crop the scanty pasture. Vincent was a homely little boy, but he had the soul of a knight-errant, and the grace of God shone from eyes that were never to lose their merry gleam even in extreme old age.

He was intelligent, too, so intelligent that the neighbors said that Jean de Paul was a fool to set such a boy to tend sheep when he had three other sons who would never be good for anything else. There was a family in the neighbor-

1

hood, they reminded him, who had had a bright boy like Vincent, and had put him to school—with what result? Why, he had taken Orders and got a benefice, and was able to support his parents now that they were getting old, besides helping his brothers to get on in the world. It was well worthwhile pinching a little for such a result as that.

Jean de Paul listened and drank in their arguments. It would be a fine thing to have a son a priest; perhaps, with luck, even a Bishop—the family fortunes would be made forever.

With a good deal of difficulty the necessary money was scraped together, and Vincent was sent to the Franciscans' school at Dax, the nearest town. There the boy made such good use of his time that four years later, when he was only sixteen, he was engaged as tutor to the children of M. de Commet, a lawyer, who had taken a fancy to the clever, hardworking young scholar. At M. de Commet's suggestion, Vincent began to study for the priesthood, while continuing the education of his young charges to the satisfaction of everybody concerned.

Five years later he took minor Orders and, feeling the need of further theological studies, set his heart on a university training and a degree. But life at a university costs money, however thrifty one may be, and although Jean de Paul sold a yoke of oxen to start his son on his career at Toulouse, at the end of a year Vincent was in difficulties. The only chance for a poor student like himself was a tutorship during the summer vacation, and here Vincent was lucky. The nobleman who engaged him was so delighted with the results that, when the vacation was over, he insisted on the young tutor taking his pupils back with him to Toulouse. There, while they attended the college, Vincent continued to direct their studies, with such success that several other noblemen confided their sons to him, and he was soon at the head of a small school.

To carry on such an establishment and to devote oneself to study at the same time was not the easiest of tasks; but Vincent was a hard and conscientious worker, and he seems to have had, even then, a strange gift of influencing others for good. For seven years he continued this double task with thorough success, completed his course of theology, took his degree, and was ordained priest in the opening years of that seventeenth century which was to be so full of consequences both for France and for himself.

Up to this time there had been nothing to distinguish Vincent from any other young student of his day. Those who knew him well respected him and loved him, and that was all. But with the priesthood came a change. From thenceforward he was to strike out a definite line of his own—a line that set him apart from the men of his time and faintly foreshadowed the Vincent of later days.

The first Mass of a newly ordained priest was usually celebrated with a certain amount of pomp and ceremony. If a cleric wanted to obtain a good living it was well to let people know that he was eligible for it; humility was not a fashionable virtue. People were therefore not a little astonished when Vincent, flatly refusing to allow any outsiders to be present, said his first Mass in a lonely little chapel in a wood near Bajet, beloved by him on account of its solitude and silence. There, entirely alone save for the acolyte and server required by the rubrics, and trembling at the thought of his own unworthiness, the newly made priest, celebrating the great Sacrifice for the first time, offered himself for life and death to be the faithful servant of his Lord. So high were his ideals of what the priestly life should be that in his saintly old age he would often say that, were he not already a priest, he would never dare to become one.

Vincent's old friend and patron, M. de Commet, was eager to do a good turn to the young cleric. He had plenty of influence and succeeded in getting him named to the rectorship of the important parish of Thil, close to the town of

Dax. This was a piece of good fortune which many would have envied; but it came to Vincent's ears that there was another claimant, who declared that the benefice had been promised to him in Rome. Rather than contest the matter in the law courts Vincent gave up the rectorship and went back to Toulouse, where he continued to teach and to study.

Some years later he was called suddenly to Bordeaux on business, and while there heard that an old lady of his acquaintance had left him all her property. This was welcome news, for Vincent was sadly in need of money, his journey to Bordeaux having cost more than he was able to pay.

On returning to Toulouse, however, he found that the prospect was not so bright as he had been led to expect. The chief part of his inheritance consisted of a debt of four or five hundred crowns owed to the old lady by a scoundrel who, as soon as he heard of her death, made off to Marseilles, thinking to escape without paying. He was enjoying life and congratulating himself on his cleverness when Vincent, to whom the sum was a little fortune, and who had determined to pursue his debtor, suddenly appeared on the scene. The thief was let off on the payment of three hundred crowns, and Vincent, thinking that he had made not too bad a bar-

gain, was preparing to return to Toulouse by
road, the usual mode of traveling in those days,
when a friend suggested that to go by sea was
not only cheaper, but more agreeable. It was
summer weather; the journey could be accom-
plished in one day; the sea was smooth; everything seemed favorable; the two friends set out
together.

A sea voyage in the seventeenth century was
by no means like a sea voyage of the present
day. There were no steamers, and vessels depended
on a favorable wind or on hard rowing. The
Mediterranean was infested with Turkish pirates,
who robbed and plundered to the very coasts of
France and Italy, carrying off the crews of captured vessels to prison or slavery.

The day that the two friends had chosen for
their journey was that of the great fair of Beau-
caire, which was famous throughout Christen-
dom. Ships were sailing backwards and forwards
along the coast with cargoes of rich goods or
the money for which they had been sold, and
the Turkish pirates were on the lookout.

The boat in which Vincent was sailing was
coasting along the Gulf of Lyons when the sailors
became aware that they were being pursued by
three Turkish brigantines. In vain they crowded
on all sail; escape was impossible. After a sharp
fight, in which all the men on Vincent's ship

were either killed or wounded—Vincent himself receiving an arrow wound the effects of which remained with him for life—the French ship was captured.

But the Turks had not come off unscathed, and so enraged were they at their losses that their first action on boarding the French vessel was to hack its unfortunate pilot into a thousand pieces. Having thus relieved their feelings, they put their prisoners in chains. But then, fearing lest the prisoners die of loss of blood and so cheat them of the money for which they meant to sell them, they bound up their wounds and went on their way of destruction and pillage. After four or five days of piracy on the high seas, they started, laden with plunder, for the coast of Barbary, noted throughout the world at that time as a stronghold of sea robbers and thieves.

Chapter 2

SLAVERY

THE pirates were bound for the port of Tunis, the largest city of Barbary. But the sight of the glittering white town with its background of mountains, set in the gorgeous coloring of the African landscape, brought no gleam of joy or comfort to the sad hearts of the prisoners. Before them lay a life of slavery which might be worse than death; there was small prospect that they would ever see their native land again.

To one faint hope, however, they clung desperately, as a drowning man clings to a straw. There was a French consul in Tunis whose business it was to look after the trade interests of his country, and it was just possible that he might use his influence to set them free.

The hope was short-lived. The pirates, expecting to make a good deal of money out of their prisoners, were equally aware of this fact, and their first act on landing was to post a notice that the captives they had for sale were Spaniards. Nothing was left to Vincent and his companions, who did not know a word of the language of the country, but to endure their cruel fate.

The Turks, having stripped their prisoners and clothed them in a kind of rough uniform, fastened chains round their necks and marched them through the town to the marketplace, where they were exhibited for sale much as cattle are at the present day. They were carefully inspected by the dealers, who looked at their teeth, felt their muscles, made them run and walk—with loads and without—to satisfy themselves that they were in good condition, and finally selected their victims. Vincent was bought by a fisherman who, finding that his new slave got hopelessly ill whenever they put out to sea, repented of his bargain and sold him to an alchemist.

In the West, as well as in the East, there were still men who believed in the Philosopher's Stone and the Elixir of Life. By means of the still undiscovered Stone they hoped to change base metals into gold, while the equally undiscovered Elixir was to prolong life indefinitely, and to make old people young.

Vincent's master was an enthusiast in his profession and kept ten or fifteen furnaces always burning in which to conduct his experiments. His slave, whose business it was to keep them alight, was kindly treated; the old man soon grew very fond of him and would harangue him by the hour on the subject of metals and essences. His great desire was that Vincent should become a Mohammedan like himself, a desire which, needless to say, remained unfulfilled, in spite of the large sums of money he promised if his slave would only oblige him in this matter.

The old alchemist, however, had a certain reputation in his own country. Having been sent for one day to the Sultan's Court, he died on the way, leaving his slave to his nephew, who lost no time in getting rid of him.

Vincent's next master was a Frenchman who had apostatized and was living as a Mohammedan on his farm in the mountains. This man had three wives, who were very kind to the poor captive—especially one of them, who, although herself a Mohammedan, was to be the cause of her husband's conversion and Vincent's release. She would go out to the fields where the Christian slave was working and bid him tell her about his country and his religion. His answers seemed to impress her greatly, and one day she asked him to sing her one of the hymns they sang in France in praise of their God.

The request brought tears to Vincent's eyes. He thought of the Israelites captive in Babylon, and of their answer to a similar demand. With an aching heart he intoned the psalm, "By the waters of Babylon," while the woman, strangely impressed by the plaintive chant, listened attentively and, when he had ended, begged for more.

The *Salve Regina* followed, and other songs of praise, after which she went home silent and thoughtful. That night she spoke to her husband. "I cannot understand," she said, "why you have given up a religion which is so good and holy. Your Christian slave has been telling me of your Faith and of your God, and has sung songs in His praise. My heart was so full of joy while he sang that I do not believe I shall be so happy even in the paradise of my fathers." Her husband, whose conscience was not quite dead within him, listened silent and abashed. "Ah," she continued, "there is something wonderful in that religion!"

The woman's words bore fruit. All day long, as her husband went about his business, the remembrance of his lost Faith was tugging at his heartstrings. Catching sight of Vincent digging in the fields, he went to him and bade him take courage. "At the first opportunity," he said, "I will escape with you to France."

It was nine long months before that opportunity came, for the Frenchman was in the Sultan's service and was not able to leave the country. At last, however, the two men, escaping together in a small boat, succeeded in reaching Avignon, and Vincent was free once more.

Cardinal Montorio, the Pope's legate, was deeply interested in the two fugitives, and a few days later reconciled the apostate, now deeply repentant, to the Church. The Cardinal, who shortly afterwards returned to Rome, took Vincent with him, showing him great kindness and introducing him to several people of importance. The opinion they formed of him is shown by the fact that he was chosen not long after to go on a secret mission to the court of Henry IV, King of France.

An interview—or rather several interviews—with a reigning monarch would have been considered in those days as a first-rate chance for anyone who had a spark of ambition. Nothing would have been easier than to put in a plea for a benefice or a bishopric; but Vincent, who was both humble and unselfish, had no thought of his own advancement. His only desire was to get his business over and to leave the Court as quickly as possible.

The question of how he was to live remaining still unanswered, he took a room in a house near one of the largest hospitals in Paris and devoted himself to the service of the sick and dying. But even the rent of the little room was more than he could afford to pay, and he was glad to share it with a companion. This was a judge from his own part of the country who was in Paris on account of a lawsuit and who, not being overburdened with money, offered to share the lodging and the rent.

It was at this time that Vincent met Father—afterwards Cardinal—de Bérulle, one of the most holy and learned priests of his time, who was occupied at that moment in founding the French Congregation of the Oratory, destined to do such good work for the clergy of France. De Bérulle was quick to recognize holiness and merit, and he and Vincent soon became fast friends.

But it did not seem to be God's will that our hero should prosper in Paris; he fell ill, and one day while he was lying in bed waiting for some medicine which had been ordered, his companion went out, leaving the cupboard in which he kept his money unlocked. The chemist's assistant, arriving shortly afterwards with the medicine and opening the cupboard to get a glass for the patient, caught sight of the purse, slipped it into his pocket, and made off.

No sooner had the judge returned than he went to the cupboard and discovered the theft. Turning furiously on the sick man, he accused him of having stolen his property and overwhelmed him with insults and abuse. Vincent, unmoved by his threats, only answered gently that he had seen nothing of the money and did not know what had become of it; but his companion, refusing to listen to reason, rushed out and accused him to the police. This led to nothing, as neither witness nor proof could be brought forward by the judge, who, furious at the failure of his accusation, went about Paris denouncing Vincent as a thief. So determined was he to ruin the poor priest whose room he had shared that he obtained an introduction to Father de Bérulle for the express purpose of making Vincent's guilt known to him. As for the latter, he bore the affront in silence, making no attempt to justify himself beyond his first declaration that he was innocent. "God knows the truth," he would reply to all accusations.

The true thief was only discovered six months later. The chemist's assistant had fallen ill and was lying at the point of death at a hospital, when, repenting of his crime, he sent to implore forgiveness of the man he had robbed. The judge, stricken with remorse, wrote at once to Vincent, offering to come and ask his pardon on his knees for the wrong he had done him.

Vincent was then living at the Oratory with Father de Bérulle, who had never doubted his innocence. He hastened to assure his old roommate that he desired no such apology and begged him to say no more about the matter. Such was his treatment of the man who had done him so grievous an injury.

It was during these years that Vincent de Paul had another strange experience in which he showed heroic courage and steadfastness. He made the acquaintance of a learned doctor of the Sorbonne who was so tormented with doubts against the Faith that his reason was in danger. This man confided his distress to Vincent, who explained to him that a temptation to doubt does not constitute unbelief, and that as long as his will remained firm he was safe. It happens, however, that such temptations often cloud the reason, and Vincent's labors to restore the man's peace of mind were in vain.

The priest, deeply moved at the sight of a soul in such danger, besought God for help, offering himself to bear the temptation in the doctor's place. It was the inspiration of a saint, and the prayer was granted. The man was instantly delivered from his doubts, which took possession of Vincent himself. The trial was long and painful. For several years this humble and fervent soul endured the agony of an incessant temptation to unbelief. But Vincent knew how to resist this most subtle snare of the Evil One, and, although the anguish was continual, his will never wavered.

Copying out the *Credo* on a small sheet of parchment, he placed it over his heart, and his only answer to the fearful doubts that harassed

him was to lay his hand upon it as he made his
act of Faith. To prevent himself from dwelling
on such thoughts, he devoted himself more than
ever to works of charity, spending himself in the
service of the sick and poor and comforting others when he himself was often in greater need
of comfort.

One day when the temptation was almost
more than he could bear and he felt himself on
the point of yielding, he made a vow to conse-
crate himself to Jesus Christ in the person of
His poor. As he made the promise the temptation vanished, and forever. His faith hencefor-
ward was a faith that had been tried and had
conquered; strong and firm as such a faith must
be, it held him ready for all that God might
send.

Chapter 3

A GREAT HOUSEHOLD

VINCENT remained two years in the house of Father de Bérulle, in the hope of obtaining permanent work. The administration of a poor country parish was, he maintained, the only thing he was fit for, but de Bérulle thought otherwise. "This humble priest," he predicted one day to a friend, "will render great service to the Church and will work much for God's glory."

St. Francis de Sales, who made Vincent's acquaintance while he was with de Bérulle, was of the same opinion. "He will be the holiest priest of his time," he said one day as he watched him. As for Vincent, he was completely won by the gentle serenity of St. Francis and took him as model in his relations with others. "I am by nature a country clod," he would say in after years, "and if I had not met the Bishop of Geneva, I should have remained a bundle of thorns all my life."

At last Vincent's desire seemed about to be fulfilled. A friend of de Bérulle's, curé of the country parish of Clichy, near Paris, announced his intention of entering the Oratory, and at de Bérulle's request chose Vincent de Paul as his successor. Here, amidst his beloved poor, Vincent was completely happy. In him the sick and the infirm found a friend such as they had never dreamed of, and any son of poor parents who showed a vocation for the priesthood was taken into the presbytery and taught by Vincent himself. The parish church, which was in great disrepair, was rebuilt; old, standing quarrels were made up; men who had not been to the Sacraments for years came back to God. Such was the influence of the Curé of Clichy that priests from the neighboring parishes came to learn the secret of his success and to ask his advice.

Vincent was looking forward to a life spent in earnest work among his people when a summons from Father de Bérulle recalled him suddenly to Paris. Nothing less than the resignation of his beloved Clichy was now asked of him by this friend to whom he owed so much. One of the greatest noblemen of France, Messire de Gondi, Count of Joigny and General of the King's Galleys, was in need of a tutor for his children and had commissioned Father de Bérulle to find him what he wanted. De Bérulle decided at once that Vincent de Paul was the man for the position and that, as he was evidently destined to do great work for God, it would be to his advantage to have powerful and influential friends.

Although the prospect of such a post filled the humble parish priest with consternation, he owed too much to de Bérulle to refuse. Setting out from Clichy with his worldly goods on a hand-barrow, he arrived at the Oratory, from whence he was to proceed to his new abode.

The house of Messire de Gondi was one of the most magnificent in Paris. The Count, one of the bravest and handsomest men of his day, was in high favor at Court; while his wife, at a time when the lives of most of the great ladies of the Court were anything but edifying, was remarkable for her fervor and piety. The de Gondi children, unfortunately, did not take after their parents, and the two boys whose education Vincent was to undertake and whose character he was to form were described by their aunt as "regular little demons." The youngest of the family, the famous, or rather infamous, Cardinal de Retz, was not yet born, but Vincent's hands were sufficiently full without him. "I should like my children to be saints rather than great noblemen," said Madame de Gondi when she presented the boys to their tutor, but the prospect seemed remote enough. The violent temper and obstinacy of his charges were a great trial to

Vincent, who used to say in later life that they had taught him, cross-grained as he was by nature, how to be gentle and patient.

The position of a man of low birth as tutor in that princely household was not without its difficulties. Vincent was a dependent; but there was a quiet dignity about him which forbade liberties. With the servants, and there were many of every grade, he was always cordial and polite, losing no chance of winning their confidence, that he might influence them for good. His duties over, he would retire to his own room, refusing, unless especially sent for, to mix with the great people who frequented the house.

Madame de Gondi, with a woman's intuition, was the first to realize the sanctity of her sons' tutor and resolved to put herself under his direction. Knowing enough of his humility to be certain that he would refuse such a request, she applied to Father de Bérulle to use his influence in the matter, and thus obtained her desire. At Vincent's suggestion she soon afterwards undertook certain works of charity, which were destined to be the seed of a great enterprise.

The Count, too, began to feel the effects of Vincent's presence in his household. It was the age of dueling, and hundreds of lives were lost in this barbarous practice. De Gondi was a famous swordsman, and although the life he led was a great deal better than that of the majority of his contemporaries, the possibility of refusing to fight when challenged, or of refraining from challenging another when his honor was at stake, had never occurred to him.

Vincent had been some time at the de Gondis' when it came to his ears that the Count intended to fight a duel on a certain day, and he resolved, if possible, to prevent it. De Gondi was present at Mass in the morning and remained on afterwards in the chapel, praying, probably, that he might prevail over his enemy.

Vincent waited till everyone had gone out, and then approached him softly. "Monsieur," he said, "I know that you intend to fight a duel; and I tell you, as a message from my Saviour, before whom you kneel, that if you do not renounce this intention His judgment will fall on you and yours." The Count, after a moment's silence, promised to give up his project, and faithfully kept his word. It was the greatest sacrifice that could have been asked of a man in de Gondi's position, and it was a thing unheard of at the time for a priest to lay down the law to a great nobleman. But the influence of sanctity is strong, and the Count was noble; for him it was the beginning of a better life.

The de Gondis usually spent part of the year at their country house in Picardy, where they had large estates. Here the love of the poor which Vincent had fostered in Madame de Gondi was in its element, and she delighted in visiting her tenants, tending the sick with her own hands, and seconding all M. Vincent's plans for their welfare.

It happened one day that Vincent was sent to the bedside of a dying peasant who had always borne a good character and was considered an excellent Christian. The man was conscious, and Vincent—moved, no doubt, by the direct inspiration of God—urged him to make a General Confession. There was much need, for he had been concealing for long years several mortal sins which he was ashamed to confess, profaning the Sacraments and deceiving all who knew him. Moved with contrition by M. Vincent's words, he confessed his crimes, acknowledging his guilt also to Madame de Gondi, who came to visit him after Vincent had departed.

"Ah, Madame," he cried, "if I had not made that General Confession my soul would have been lost for all eternity!"

The incident made a lasting impression on both Vincent and the Countess. Here was a man who for years had been living in deceit and making an unworthy use of the Sacraments. How many others might be in like case! It was a terrible thought. "Ah, Monsieur Vincent," cried the great lady, "how many souls are being lost! Can you do nothing to help them?"

Her words found an echo in Vincent's heart. Next Sunday he preached a sermon in the parish church on the necessity of General Confession. It was the first of the famous mission sermons destined to do so much good in France. While he spoke, Madame de Gondi prayed, and the result far surpassed their expectations. So great were the crowds that flocked to Confession that Vincent was unable to cope with them and had to apply to the Jesuits at Amiens for help. The other villages on the estate were visited in turn, with equal success. Vincent used to look back in later life to this first mission sermon as the beginning of his work for souls.

The result of all this for the preacher, however, was a certain prestige, and his humility took alarm. Monsieur and Madame de Gondi now treated their sons' tutor with the reverence due to a saint. His name was on the lips of everybody; and yet, as Vincent sadly acknowledged to himself, the work for which he had been engaged was a failure. The "little demons" were as headstrong and violent as ever; it was only on their parents that he had been able to make any impression.

Fearful of being caught in the snare of worldly honors, he resolved to seek safety in flight. Father de Bérulle had sent him to the house of Monsieur de Gondi; to him did he appeal in his distress. His work as a tutor had been a failure, he told him; he could do nothing with his pupils, and he was receiving honor which he in no way deserved. He ended by begging to be allowed to work for the poor in some humble and lonely place, and de Bérulle decided to grant his wish. The country parish of Châtillon was in need of workers, was the answer; let him go there and exercise his zeal for souls.

The only remaining difficulty was to get away from the great house. Dreading the outcry that he knew would follow the announcement of his resolution, and the arguments that would be used against him, Vincent departed, declaring simply that personal affairs called him away from Paris.

Only when he had been already established for some time in his new parish did it dawn on the de Gondis that his absence was not to be merely temporary. They were in desperation. Madame de Gondi did nothing but weep, while her husband applied to everyone whom he thought to have any influence with Vincent to persuade him to return. "If he has not the gift of teaching children," he wrote to a friend, "it does not matter; he shall have a tutor to work under him. He shall live exactly as he likes if he will only come back. Get de Bérulle to persuade him. I shall be a good man some day," ends this great nobleman pathetically, "if only he will stay with me."

Chapter 4

THE GALLEYS

M. DE BÉRULLE had certainly not exaggerated matters when he said that the parish of Châtillon-les-Dombes was in need of earnest workers. Vincent looked about him and set to work at once.

The first thing to be done was to clean out the church, which was in such a state of dirt and squalor that people had some excuse for not wishing to enter it. He then turned his attention to the clergy already there. They were ignorant and easygoing men, for the most part, who thought a good deal more of their own amusement than of the needs of their flock, but they were not bad at heart. Vincent's representations of what a priest's life ought to be astonished them at first and convinced them later—all the more so in that they saw in him the very ideal that he strove to set before them.

There was no presbytery at Châtillon, and to the astonishment of everyone, Vincent hired a lodging in the house of a young gentleman who had the reputation of being one of the most riotous livers in the town. He was, moreover, half a heretic, and Vincent had been warned to have nothing to do with him. But the new rector had his own ideas on the subject, and the ill-assorted pair soon became very good friends.

The change in the young man's mode of life was gradual. His first step was to be reconciled to the Church, his second to begin to interest himself in the poor. Gradually his bad companions dropped away, until one day Châtillon suddenly awoke to the fact that this most rackety of individuals was taking life seriously—was, in fact, a changed man. The whole town was in a stir. Who was this priest who had so suddenly come among them, so self-forgetful, so simple, so unassuming, yet whose influence was so strong with all classes?

It was a question that might well be asked in the light of what was yet to come.

There lived near Châtillon a certain Count de Rougemont, a noted duelist, whose violence and immorality were the talk of the neighborhood. Having heard people speak of the wonderful eloquence of M. Vincent, this man came one day out of curiosity to hear him preach. Surprised and touched in spite of himself, he determined to make the preacher's acquaintance and, hastening into his presence, flung himself on his knees before him.

"I am a wretch and a sinner!" he cried, "but tell me what to do and I will do it." Raising him with gentle courtesy, Vincent bade him take courage, and spoke to him of all the good that a man of his position might do in the world. The Count, profoundly struck by the contrast between this man's life and his own—the one so powerful for good, and the other so strong for evil—vowed to mend his ways. And he kept his word.

One by one he sold his estates to find the wherewithal for Vincent's schemes of charity, and he would have stripped himself of all that he had, had not Vincent himself forbidden it. His sword, which had served him in all his duels, and to which he was very much attached, he broke in pieces on a rock. His great chateau, the walls of which had rung to the sound of wild carousals, was now thrown open to the sick and the poor, whom the once-dreaded Count insisted on serving with his own hands. He died the death of a saint a few years later, amid the blessings of all the people whom he had helped.

The ladies of the parish, to whom before Vincent's arrival the hour of the Sunday Mass had seemed too long for God's service and who had spent it chattering behind their fans, began also to realize that there was something in life besides selfish amusement. Some of them, moved by curiosity, went to see the new preacher, who, receiving them with his usual kindness and courtesy, drew a touching picture of the suffering and poverty that surrounded them and begged them to think sometimes of their less fortunate brothers and sisters.

Two of the richest and most fashionable ladies of the district, touched by Vincent's words and example, gave themselves up entirely to the service of the poor, traveling about the country nursing the sick, and even risking their lives in the care of the plague-stricken. They were the forerunners of those "Sisters of Charity" who were in after years to carry help and comfort among the poor of every country.

One day, as Vincent was about to say Mass, one of these ladies begged him to speak to the congregation in favor of a poor family whose members were sick and starving. So successful was his appeal that when he himself went a few hours later to see what could be done, he found the road thronged with people carrying food and necessaries.

This, Vincent at once realized, was not practical. There would be far too much today and nothing tomorrow. There was no want of charity, but it needed organization. Sending for the two ladies, he explained to them a scheme which he had thought out on his way home. Those who were ready to help the poor were to band themselves together, each in turn promising to provide a day's food for starving families.

Thus was founded the first confraternity of the "Ladies of Charity," who were to work in concert for the relief of their poorer brethren. The association was to be under the management of the curé of the parish, and every good woman might belong to it. Its members were to devote themselves to the service of the poor for the love of Our Lord Jesus Christ, their Patron. They were to tend the sick cheerfully and kindly, as they would their own children, not disdaining to minister to them with their own hands. The work developed quickly; confraternities of charity were soon adopted in nearly all the parishes of France and have since extended over the whole Christian world.

The de Gondis, in the meantime, had discovered the place of Vincent's retreat and had written him several letters, piteously urging him to return. They had succeeded in enlisting as their advocate a certain M. du Fresne, a friend of Vincent's, who had promised to plead their cause and who set about it with a shrewd common sense that was not without its effect.

The work at Châtillon, he represented to Vincent, could be carried on by any good priest now that it had been set agoing, whereas in refusing to return to the de Gondis he was neglecting an opportunity for doing good on a very much larger scale. Helped by their money and their influence, not only their vast estates, but Paris itself, lay open to him as a field for his labors. Moreover, he had taken his own way in going to Châtillon; was he sure that it was God's way?

Vincent was humble enough to believe that he might be in the wrong. He consented to go to Paris to see M. de Bérulle and to allow himself to be guided by his advice. The result was a foregone conclusion, for the de Gondis had won over de Bérulle completely to their side. The next day Vincent returned to the Hôtel de Gondi, where he promised to remain during the lifetime of the Countess.

Delighted to have him back at any price, Vincent's noble patrons asked for nothing better than to further all his schemes for the welfare of the poor and infirm. Confraternities of charity like that of Châtillon were established on all the de Gondi estates, Madame de Gondi herself setting the example of what a perfect Lady of Charity should be. Neither dirt, discourtesy nor risk of infection could discourage this earnest disciple of Vincent. In spite of weak health she gave freely of her time, her energy and her money.

M. de Gondi was, as we have already seen, General of the King's Galleys, or, as we should now say, Admiral of the Fleet. It was no easy post in days when the Mediterranean was infested with Turkish pirates, to whom the royal ships had to give frequent chase; but the General had distinguished himself more than once by his skill and courage at this difficult task.

The use of steam was as yet unknown, and the King's galleys were rowed by the convicts and prisoners of France, for it would have been impossible to find volunteers for the work. Chained to their oars night and day, kept in order by cruel cuts of the lash on their bare shoulders, these men lived and died on the rowers' bench without spiritual help or assistance of any kind. The conditions of service were such that many prisoners took their own lives rather than face the torments of such an existence.

As Vincent went about his works of charity in Paris it occurred to him to visit the dungeons where the men who had been condemned to the galleys were confined. What he saw filled him with horror. Huddled together in damp and filthy prisons, crawling with vermin, covered with sores and ulcers, brawling, blaspheming and fighting, the galley slaves made a picture suggestive only of Hell.

Vincent hastened to M. de Gondi and, trembling with emotion, poured forth a description of the horrors he had seen.

"These are your people, Monseigneur!" he cried; "you will have to answer for them before God." The General was aghast; it had never occurred to him to think of the condition of the men who rowed his ships, and he gladly gave Vincent a free hand to do whatever he could to relieve them.

Calling two other priests to his assistance, Vincent set to work at once to visit the convicts in the Paris prisons; but the men were so brutalized that it was difficult to know how to win them. The first advances were met with cursing and blasphemy, but Vincent was not to be discouraged. With his own gentle charity he performed the lowest offices for these poor wretches to whom his heart went out with such an ardent pity; he cleansed them from the vermin which infested them and dressed their neglected sores. Gradually they were softened and would listen while he spoke to them of the Saviour who had died to save their souls. At Vincent's earnest request, money was collected among his friends and patrons, and a hospital built where the prisoners condemned to the galleys might be nursed into good health before they went on board.

In due time the rumor of the good work that was being done reached the ears of Louis XIII,

who promptly made Vincent de Paul Almoner
to the King's ships, with the honors and privi-
leges of a naval officer and a salary of six hundred livres. This enabled Vincent to carry his
mission farther afield, and he determined to visit
all the convict prisons in the seaport towns, taking Marseilles as his first station.

Here, where the conditions were perhaps even
worse than in Paris, Vincent met them in the
same spirit and conquered by the same means.
The fact that he had once been a slave himself
gave him an insight into the sufferings of the
galley slaves and a wonderful influence over them.
Accustomed as they were to be looked upon as
brutes, it was a new experience to be treated as
if it were a privilege to be in their company.
This strange new friend who went about among
them, kissing their chains, sympathizing with
their sufferings and attending to their lowest
needs seemed to them like an Angel from Heaven;
even the most hardened could not resist such
treatment.

In the meantime, through the generosity of
Vincent's friends, hospitals were being built and
men and women were offering themselves to
help in any capacity in this work of charity.
Many of these earnest Christians gave their very
lives for the galley slaves; for fevers, plague and
contagious diseases of every kind raged in the

filthy convict prisons, and many priests and lay helpers died of the infection. Yet other devoted workers were always found to take their place, and the work which Vincent had inaugurated thrived and prospered.

Idealized painting of St. Vincent de Paul
preaching to the galley slaves.

Chapter 5

MISSION WORK

THE incident which had given rise to Vincent's first mission at Folleville had never been forgotten by Madame de Gondi. It seemed to her that there was need to multiply such missions among the country poor, and no sooner had Vincent returned to her house than she offered him a large sum of money to endow a band of priests who would devote their lives to evangelizing the peasantry on her estates.

Vincent was delighted, but considering himself unfit to undertake the management of such an enterprise, he proposed that it should be put into the hands of the Jesuits or the Oratorians.

Madame de Gondi, although convinced in her own mind that Vincent, and Vincent alone, was the man to carry out the enterprise, obediently suggested it to one religious Order after another. In every case some obstacle intervened, until the Countess was more than ever persuaded that her first instinct had been right. Knowing Vincent's loyalty to Holy Church and

his obedience to authority, she determined to
have recourse to her brother-in-law, the Archbishop of Paris. An old house called the Collège des Bons Enfants was at that moment
vacant. She asked it of the Archbishop, whom
she had interested in her scheme, and who proposed to Vincent to undertake the foundation.
There was no longer room for hesitation; the
will of God seemed plain; indeed, Vincent's
love of the poor had been for some time strug-
gling with his humility.

The new Congregation was to consist of a
few good priests who, renouncing all thought of
honor and worldly advancement, were to devote
their lives to preaching in the villages and small
towns of France. Their traveling expenses were
to be paid from a common fund. They were to
spend themselves in the service of their neighbor, instructing, catechizing and exhorting; and
they were to take nothing in return for their
labors. Nine months of the year were to be given
to this kind of work; the other three to prayer
and preparation.

In March, 1625, the foundation was made,
and Vincent de Paul was named the first superior. It was stipulated, however, that he should
remain, as he had already promised, in the house
of the founders, a condition which seemed likely
to doom the enterprise to failure. Vincent could

hardly fail to realize how necessary it was that
the superior of a new Congregation should be
in residence in his own house, but he confided
the little company to God and awaited the devel-
opment of events.

The solution was altogether unexpected. Two
months after the signing of the contract of foundation, Madame de Gondi was taken suddenly
ill, and she died a few days later. Her broken-
hearted husband not only consented to Vincent's
residence in the Collège des Bons Enfants, but
shortly afterwards, leaving that world where he
had shone so brilliantly, he himself became a
postulant at the Oratory.

The beginnings of the new Congregation were
humble enough. Its members were three in number: Vincent, his friend M. Portail, and a poor
priest who had lately joined them. Before setting out on their mission journeys they used
to give the key of the house to a neighbor; but
as there was nothing in it to steal, there was
little cause for anxiety. In the course of their
travels other priests, realizing the greatness of
the work, asked to be enrolled in the little company. Its growth, nevertheless, was slow; ten
years after the foundation the Congregation
only numbered thirty-three members; but Vincent had no desire that it should be otherwise.
In 1652 it was recognized by Pope Urban VIII

under the name of the Congregation of the Mission.

Vincent lavished the greatest care on the training of his priests. They were to be simple and frank in their relations with the poor, modest in manner, friendly and easy of access.

"Our sermons must go straight to the point," he would say, "so that the humblest of our hearers may understand; our language must be clear and unaffected." The love of virtue and the hatred of evil were the points to be insisted on; the people were to be shown where virtue lay and how to attain it. For "fine sermons" Vincent had the greatest contempt; he would use his merry wit to make fun of the pompous preachers whose only thought was to impress their audience with an idea of their own eloquence.

"Of what good is a display of rhetoric?" he would ask; "who is the better for it? It serves no purpose but self-advertisement."

The Mission Priests did good wherever they went; everybody wanted them, and it was hard to satisfy the appeals for missions which came from all over the country. In due time the Congregation outgrew the Collège des Bons Enfants, and was transferred to a large Augustinian priory which had originally been a leper hospital, and still bore the name of St. Lazare.*

Up to this time the Mission Priests had contented themselves with ministering to the peasantry, but in the course of their travels it had become painfully apparent that the clergy themselves were in urgent need of some awakening force. Those of good family led, for the most part, worldly and frivolous lives, while the humbler sort were as ignorant as the peasants among whom they lived. The religious wars had led to laxity and carelessness; drunkenness and vice were fearfully prevalent.

To Vincent, with his high ideals of the priesthood, this was a terrible revelation. The old custom of giving a retreat to priests who were about to be ordained had fallen into disuse. With the assistance of some of the French bishops he determined to revive it, and retreats of ten or fourteen days were organized at St. Lazare for candidates to the priesthood. Here, in an atmosphere of prayer and recollection, those who were about to be ordained had every opportunity of realizing the greatness of the step that they were taking and of making resolutions for their future lives.

---

*The name *St. Lazare* (French for "St. Lazarus") led to St. Vincent de Paul's congregation becoming known as the *Lazarists*. The members are also known as the *Vincentians*; their official title in the U.S. today is the *Congregation of the Mission (C.M.).—Publisher*, 1998.

The Mission Priests were to help in this work more by example than by precept; they were to preach by humility and simplicity. "It is not by knowledge that you will do them good," Vincent often repeated, "or by the fine things you say, for they are more learned than you—they have read or heard it all before. It is by what they see of your lives that you will help them; if you yourselves are striving for perfection, God will use you to lead these gentlemen in the right way."

The blessing of God seemed, indeed, to rest upon the ordination retreats; nearly all who made them carried away something of Vincent's noble ideal of the priestly life. Many, to whom they had been the turning point of a lifetime, felt the need of further help and instruction from the man who had awakened all that was noblest in their natures.

To meet this necessity Vincent inaugurated a kind of guild for young priests who desire to live worthy of their vocation. Weekly gatherings were held at St. Lazare under the name of "Tuesday Conferences," where difficulties were discussed, debates held and counsels given. It was not easy to belong to the "Conferences." Members were pledged to offer their lives completely to God and to renounce all self-interest. Nevertheless, they increased rapidly in number, and the Conferences were attended by all the most influential priests in Paris.

But Vincent's zeal was boundless, and one good work grew out of another. The retreats for ordination candidates having been so successful, he conceived the idea of giving retreats on the same lines for the laity. The work thrived beyond all expectation. All were admitted without exception: noblemen and beggars, young men and old, the learned and the ignorant, priests and laymen. St. Lazare at such times, Vincent once said, was like Noah's ark: every kind of creature was to be found in it.

The only difficulty was the expense entailed, for many of the retreatants could pay nothing toward their board and lodging, and Vincent would refuse nobody. Here, as in so many other cases, it was the Congregation of the Ladies of Charity, founded by Vincent in Paris, that came nobly to his rescue. There was Madame de Maignelais, sister of M. de Gondi, who, left a widow at the age of twenty, devoted herself and her enormous fortune to alms and good works. There was the Duchesse d'Aiguillon, niece of the great Richelieu; Madame de Miramion, beautiful and pious; Madame Goussault, the first President of the Dames de Charité; and many others, whose purses were always at Vincent's disposal.

The Congregation of the Mission Priests was to inaugurate another good work for which there was an urgent necessity in the world of Vincent's day. While yet at the Collège des Bons Enfants, he had realized how great was the need of a special training for young men destined for the priesthood and had founded a small seminary. After the move to St. Lazare the undertaking had grown and prospered. A college of the same kind had been lately founded by M. Olier, the zealous curé of St. Sulpice; and these two institutions, the first of the famous seminaries which were later to spread all over France, were powerful for the reform of the clergy. One hundred and fifty years later the Mission Priests of St. Lazare alone were at the head of sixty such seminaries.

So the work of the Congregation increased and multiplied until it seemed almost too much for human capacity. But Vincent knew wherein lay the strength of the Mission Priests. "How may we hope to do our work?" he would ask. "How can we lead souls to God? How can we stem the tide of wickedness among the people? Let us realize that this is not man's work at all, it is God's. Human energy will only hinder it unless directed by God. The most important point of all is that we should be in touch with Our Lord in prayer."

Dearest to his heart of all his undertakings was the first and chief work of the Congregation—the holding of missions for the poor. By twos and threes he would send out his sons to their labors, bidding them travel to their destination in the cheapest possible way. They were to accept neither free quarters nor gifts of any kind. All their thoughts and prayers were to be concentrated on their work: they were to live for their mission. Two sermons were to be preached daily—simple instructions on the great truths—and those who had not yet made their First Communion were to be catechized. The mission lasted ten or fourteen days, during which the Mission Priests were to have as much personal contact with the people as possible, visiting the sick and the infirm, reconciling enemies and showing themselves as the friends of all.

It was no easy task to be a good Mission Priest. It meant self-mastery, self-renunciation, self-forgetfulness total and complete. It meant the laying aside of much that lies very close to a man's heart. "Unless the Congregation of the Mission is humble," said Vincent, "and realizes that it can accomplish nothing of any value, but that it is more apt to mar than to make, it will never be of much effect; but when it has this spirit it will be fit for the purposes of God."

Yet, in spite of all that such a vocation meant

of self-renunciation, year after year the Mission Priests increased in number. "This work is not human, it is from God," was Vincent's answer to those who marvelled at the power of the company for good.

Chapter 6

THE GREY SISTERS

A LTHOUGH many of the great ladies of Paris had enrolled themselves among the Ladies of Charity and were ready to help Vincent to the utmost of their ability, much of the work to be done in that great town was hardly within their scope. The care of the sick in the hospitals alone demanded ceaseless labor and an amount of time which few wives and mothers could give. There was a gap which needed filling, as Vincent could not but see, and he took immediate steps to fill it.

The instrument he required lay close to his hand in the person of Louise le Gras, a widow lady who had devoted her life to the service of the poor. She had gathered in her house a few young working women from the country to help her in her labors; these were the people needed to step in where the Ladies of Charity fell short. A larger house was taken on the outskirts of Paris; good country girls who were ready to give their services without payment were encouraged to devote themselves to the work, and Louise le Gras, with all the enthusiasm of her unselfish nature, set to work to train the little company to efficiency.

Of one thing this holy woman was absolutely convinced—unless the motive with which the work was undertaken was supernatural, neither perseverance nor success could be expected. "It is of little use for us to run about the streets with bowls of soup," she would say, "if we do not make the love of God the object of our effort. If we let go of the thought that the poor are His members, our love for them will soon grow cold." To pray, to labor and to obey was to be the whole duty of the members of the little sisterhood. The strength of their influence was to be the fact that it was Christ to whom they ministered in the person of His poor.

To many of these girls, rough and ignorant as they were for the most part, life in a great town was full of dangers. Such work as theirs could only be adequately done by women whose lives were consecrated to God, who were prepared to spend themselves without stint or measure in His service. "If you aspire to perfection, you must learn to die to self" was the teaching of their foundress.

Louise le Gras was a soul of prayer, and she knew that more was needed than fervent phil-

St. Vincent and the Sisters of Charity.

anthropy and a heart full of pity to give the Sisters courage for the lives they had undertaken to lead. Uncloistered nuns were at that time a thing unheard of, and in the first days of the little company the Sisters were often greeted with insults when they appeared in the streets. In Vincent's own words, they were "a community who had no monastery but the houses of the sick, no cells but a lodging of the poorest room, no cloisters but the streets, no grille but the fear of God, and no veil but their own modesty."

Their life was hard. They rose at four, their food was of the plainest description, they spent their days in an unhealthy atmosphere and were habitually overworked. The life of a true Sister of Charity needed to be rooted and nourished in the love of God, and no one realized it more completely than Vincent himself. In his weekly conferences, when they met together at St. Lazare, he would set before them the ideals of their vocation, bidding them above all things to be humble and simple.

"You see, my sisters," he would say to them, "you are only rough country girls, brought up like myself to keep the flocks." He understood their temptations and knew their weaknesses, but the standard was never to be lowered.

"The Daughters of Charity must go wherever they are needed," he said, "but this obligation exposes them to many temptations, and therefore they have special need of strictness." They were never to pay a visit unless it was part of their work; they were never to receive one; they were not to stand talking in the street unless it was absolutely necessary; they were never to go out without leave.

"What?" Vincent makes them say in one of his conferences, "do you ask me to be my own enemy, to be forever denying myself, to do everything I have no wish to do, to destroy self altogether?"

"Yes, my sisters," he answers; "and unless you do so, you will be slipping back in the way of righteousness." Their lives were of necessity full of temptations, and only in this spirit could they resist them.

Life in the streets of a great city was full of interest to these country girls, and it required a superhuman self-control to go about with downcast eyes, noticing nothing. At the weekly conference one of the Sisters acknowledged that if she passed a troop of mountebanks or a peepshow, the desire to look was so strong upon her that she could only resist it by pressing her crucifix to her heart and repeating, "O Jesus, Thou art worth it all."

One day Vincent appeared among them in great joy. He had just met a gentleman in the street, who had said to him, "Monsieur, today I saw two of your daughters carrying food to the sick, and so great was the modesty of one of them that she never even raised her eyes."

It was many years before he would allow the Sisters, however great their desire, to bind themselves by vows to the service of Christ in His poor. When at last the permission was given, the formula of the vows, which were taken for one year only, ran thus:

"I, the undersigned, in the Presence of God, renew the promises of my Baptism, and make the vow of poverty, of chastity, and of obedience to the Venerable Superior General of the Priests of the Mission in the Company of the Sisters of Charity, that I may bind myself all this year to the service, bodily and spiritual, of the poor and sick—our masters. And this by the aid of God, which I ask through His Son Jesus Christ Crucified, and through the prayers of the Holy Virgin."

Although vows taken thus annually did not imply a lifelong dedication, the Sisters of Charity who returned to the world were few. Many heroic women spent their lives, unknown and unnoticed, in the daily drudgery of nursing the sick or trying to maintain order in country hospitals.

"The saintliness of a Daughter of Charity,"

said Vincent, "rests on faithful adherence to the Rule; on faithful service to the nameless poor; in love and charity and pity; in faithful obedience to the doctor's orders . . . It keeps us humble to be quite ordinary . . ."

"For the greater honor of Our Lord, their Master and Patron," runs a certain passage in their Rule, "the Sisters of Charity shall have in everything they do a definite intention to please Him, and shall try to conform their life to His, especially in His poverty, His humility, His gentleness, His simplicity and austerity." Therein was to lie their strength and the secret of their courage; before them stood their crucified Lord, bidding them suffer and be strong.

The "Grey Sisters," as they were called by the poor, not only nursed in the hospitals of Paris, but went far and wide on their errands of mercy. Scarcely a day passed without an appeal. After the siege of Arras in 1656, Louise le Gras was implored to send help to those of the inhabitants who had survived the horrors of the war. Only two Sisters could be spared to meet the requirements of eight parishes; dirt, disease and famine reigned supreme; yet one of them, writing to her Superior to tell her that the other had been obliged to stop working from sheer exhaustion, says: "I have never heard a word of complaint from her lips or seen anything in her face but perfect content."

A little later the Sisters were sent for to nurse the wounded soldiers in the hospitals of Calais. "My dear daughters," said Vincent, as he bade them farewell, "be sure that, wherever you go, God will take care of you."

Only four could be spared, and the soldiers were dying in scores of an infectious disease. It was at the risk of their lives that the Sisters went among them, and two out of the four caught the infection and died. When the news reached Paris, there were numbers eager to take their place, and the four who were chosen set off rejoicing.

The hospitals all over the country were in need of reform, and in Paris every new scheme for the relief of the poor called for the Sisters' assistance. In the hospital at Marseilles they were tending the convicts; when the home for the aged poor was instituted, it was under their government; the Foundling Hospital was in their hands. Wherever there was need for zeal and self-denial, there these devoted women were to be found, ready to lay down their lives in the service of their neighbor. They had renounced what pleasures the world might hold for them for a life of toil and discomfort; their sacrifice was hidden; they lived and died unnoticed.

"We have no knowledge of our way except

that we follow Jesus," writes the Mother and Foundress of the company, "always working and always suffering. He could never have led us unless His own resolve had taken Him as far as death on the Cross."

In 1641 the Sisters of Charity had taken up a fresh work, one which lay very close to Vincent's heart, the teaching of little children. It should be, he told them, as much a part of their vocation as the care of the poor and the sick, and they were to spare no pains to give these little creatures the solid Christian teaching which nothing can replace.

As the years went on, many ladies of noble birth enrolled themselves in the company, working side by side with their humbler sisters in the relief of every kind of misery; but daughter of peer or of peasant, the Sister of Charity was and is, before all else, the daughter of God and the servant of the poor. Louise le Gras rejoiced one day when she heard that one of the Sisters had been severely beaten by a patient and had borne it without a murmur. She, their Superior, and a woman of gentle birth, led the way in that humility which was their strength. She had been trained by Vincent de Paul and had learned from a living model.

Chapter 7

THE FOUNDLINGS

M. VINCENT was passing one day through the streets of Paris on one of his errands of mercy when he saw a beggar mutilating a new-born baby in order to expose it to the public as an object of pity. Snatching the poor little creature out of the hands of its tormentor, Vincent carried it to the "Couche St. Landry," an institution which had been founded for the care of children left homeless and deserted in the streets.

The state of things in that household filled him with horror. The "Couche" was managed by a widow, who, helped by two servants, received about four hundred children within the year. These unfortunate little creatures, in a state of semi-starvation and utter neglect, were crowded together into two filthy holes, where the greater number died of pestilence. Of those who survived, some were drugged with laudanum to silence their cries, while others were put an end to by any other method that suggested itself to the wretched women into whose hands they had fallen.

The sight of the "Couche" was one that could not fail to rouse any mother's heart to indignation. Vincent took one or two of the Ladies of Charity to the place and let them judge for themselves. The result was a resolve to rescue the little victims at any cost.

It was not difficult to get possession of the babies; their inhuman guardians were in the habit of selling them for the modest sum of one franc each to anyone who would take them off their hands. But the cost of maintenance was a more serious matter. A house was taken near the Collège des Bons Enfants, and twelve of the miserable little victims were ransomed and installed there under the care of Louise le Gras and the Sisters of Charity.

But this was only a beginning. The work appealed all the more strongly to the Ladies of Charity for the reason that most of the babies were unbaptized. It was a question of saving souls as well as bodies, and every effort was made to empty the Couche. The Ladies, often at the cost of real self-denial, gave every penny they could afford; Louis XIII and his Queen, Anne of Austria, contributed liberally. In ten years' time Vincent's institution had grown to such an extent that it was able to open its doors to all the foundlings in Paris.

Four thousand children had been adopted and

cared for, and the numbers were still increasing; finances had been stretched to the breaking point; there came a moment when it seemed impossible to meet the expenses any longer. The Thirty Years' War was raging, and the eastern provinces of France, which had served as a battlefield for the nations, were reduced to the utmost misery. There were many other claims on the purses of the Ladies of Charity; the time had come when it looked as if there was nothing to be done but sorrowfully give up an undertaking that was altogether beyond their power.

But the very thought of such a possibility nearly broke Vincent's heart; he determined to make one last effort, and, gathering the Ladies together, laid the case before them in all simplicity.

"I ask of you to say only one word," he said to them: "will you go on with the work or no? You are perfectly free; you are bound by no promise. Yet, before you decide, reflect for one moment on what you have done, and what you are doing. Your loving care has preserved the lives of a very great number of children, who without your help would have been lost in time as well as eternity; for these innocent creatures have learned to know and serve God as soon as they were able to speak. Some of them are beginning to work and to be self-supporting. Does not so good a beginning promise yet better results?

"Ladies, it was pity and charity that moved you to adopt these little ones as your children. You were their mothers by grace when their mothers by nature had deserted them. Are you going to abandon them now? If you cease to be their mothers you become their judges; their lives are in your hands. I will now ask you to give your votes: it is time for you to give sentence and to make up your minds that you have no longer any mercy to spare for them. If in your charity you continue to take care of them, they will live; if not, they will certainly die. It is impossible to deny what your own experience must tell you is true."

Vincent paused; his voice was trembling with emotion; he was answered by the tears of the assembly. It was decided that at any cost the Foundling Hospital must be supported. The work was saved. The practical question of expenses, however, remained yet to be faced, and although the King increased his subscription, the funds were still insufficient. But the Ladies made still greater sacrifices; the Sisters of Charity limited themselves to one meal a day, and Vincent, who had already reduced himself to the direst poverty, strained every nerve to help.

The Foundling Hospital was thus kept going

until some years after Vincent's death, when the State took over the responsibility, and the work ceased to depend on voluntary support.

Of all the good works on which he had spent himself, this was the one, it is said, that appealed to him the most strongly. He knew every baby in the Foundling Hospital by name; the death of any one of them caused him a very real sorrow, and he would appear among them at the most unexpected hours. Their innocence and happiness rejoiced him, and he delighted in watching their pretty baby ways. At the sight of his kind, homely face, they would gather round him, clinging to his hands or his cassock, certain of a smile or a caress. He came across much that was neither innocent nor attractive in his dealings with the world; he was one who never judged harshly, and who could always see in man, however depraved, the image of his Maker; yet the innocence and purity of his own soul found their best solace in the company of these little creatures whom he had rescued from a double death. They were his recreation in the moments of depression which all who work for the welfare of mankind must experience and which are more intense in proportion as the zeal is stronger.

He was blamed one day, when the difficulty of providing for the foundlings was at its height, for having spent upon them alms destined for the support of the Mission.

"Ah!" he cried, "do you think Our Lord will be less good to us because we put the welfare of these poor children before our own? Since that merciful Saviour said to His disciples, 'Suffer the little children to come unto Me,' can we who wish to follow Him reject these babies when they come to us?"

But if the foundlings had a large share of Vincent's heart, it was great enough for all who were in suffering or distress. The misery in the provinces of Lorraine and Picardy was hardly to be described; the people were literally dying of hunger. The Ladies of Charity had at first come nobly to the rescue, but the Foundling Hospital was now absorbing all their funds; they could do no more. Then Vincent conceived the idea of printing leaflets describing the sufferings of the people and what was being done to help them by the Mission Priests. These were sold at the church doors, in the public squares and in the streets, and people bought them with such avidity that Vincent soon realized a steady little income.

In days when there were no such things as newspapers, regular tidings from the provinces were as welcome as they were unexpected. "God showered such blessings on the work," says Vincent, "that the greater number of those who read these narratives opened their hands for the relief of the poor."

The next step was to institute in all the regions where famine was prevalent public soup kitchens, where nourishing soup, made at the lowest possible cost, was portioned out among the poor. Vincent himself gave minute directions for its making, prescribing the ingredients so that the greatest number of people might be maintained at the least expense.

In many places laid waste by fire and sword, the dead remained unburied for days or even weeks. Heaps of filth and garbage were left to rot at the doors of houses and in the streets; pestilence and fever reigned supreme. Here, again, the Priests of the Mission and the Sisters of Charity devoted themselves to the work that no one else would do. Organizing themselves into bands, they went about burying the dead, nursing the sick and cleansing the streets, many of them dying of the pestilence.

It was very necessary, moreover, to take steps to bring back some kind of prosperity to the devastated country. Seeds and grain were distributed among the peasants, who were encouraged to cultivate the land and taught the best methods of doing so. All these different undertakings were carried out with the regularity and practical common sense that were characteristic of the sons of St. Vincent de Paul, accustomed as they were to brave hardship and danger without a thought of their own safety.

If their Superior asked much of others, he himself set the example in generosity. It was said of him that he never could keep anything for his own use, either clothes or money; everything that came into his hands went straight to the poor. There were days at St. Lazare when it seemed uncertain where the daily bread was to come from, or whether it was to come at all; but Vincent put his trust in God, who never failed him, and he gave while there was anything to give.

Several times, while he was organizing relief for the eastern provinces, his heart almost failed him at the magnitude of the work he had undertaken, and it was at one of these moments that he dared to face the terrible Richelieu, to demand peace in the name of the suffering people.

"Monseigneur!" he cried, appearing before the great Cardinal with tears streaming down his cheeks, "give us peace! Have pity on France and give us peace." Richelieu's heart was certainly none of the softest, but even he seems to have been touched by this earnest appeal. At all events, he showed no anger.

"I wish for peace," he declared, "and I am

taking means to procure it, but it does not depend on me alone"; and he dismissed Vincent with an unwonted urbanity. His was not the only hard nature that was softened by contact with St. Vincent de Paul. The love of this man for his fellow men was infectious, for it was born of his love for Christ.

von Hackel, 1890 *Sisters of Charity, Augsburg*

St. Vincent, Sisters of Charity and foundlings.

Chapter 8

AT COURT

WHEN Louis XIII was on his deathbed, with all the Bishops and Archbishops of France ready to offer him their services, it was M. Vincent, the humble Mission Priest, who prepared him to meet his God. During the last days of the King's life, Vincent never left him, and in his arms Louis XIII breathed his last. Then, having done the work for which he had come, Vincent slipped quietly out of the palace to hasten back to St. Lazare and his beloved poor.

Some remarks made by the King during his illness and certain other words of Vincent's were remembered by the Queen, Anne of Austria, who had been left Regent during the minority of her son. Richelieu was dead, and Mazarin, his pupil, a crafty and unscrupulous Italian, had succeeded him as chief Minister of State. His influence over the Queen was growing daily, but it was not yet strong enough to override all her scruples. She was a good-natured woman, quite ready to do right when it was not too inconvenient, and it was clear to her that of late years bishoprics and abbeys had been too often given to most unworthy persons. In France the Crown was almost supreme in such matters; the Queen therefore determined to appoint a "Council of Conscience" consisting of five members, whose business it would be to help her with advice as to ecclesiastical preferment.

Mazarin's astonishment and disgust when he heard that Vincent de Paul had been appointed one of the number were as great as Vincent's own consternation. The responsibility and the difficulties which he would have to face filled the humble Mission Priest with the desire to escape such an honor at any price; he even applied to the Queen in person to beg her to reconsider her decision.

But Anne was obdurate, and Vincent was forced to yield. "I have never been more worthy of compassion or in greater need of prayers than now," he wrote to one of his friends, and his forebodings were not without cause. If Mazarin had been unable to prevent the Queen from naming Vincent as one of the Council of Conscience, he had at least succeeded in securing his own nomination. In the cause of honesty and justice, and for the Church's welfare, the Superior of St. Lazare would have to contend with the foremost statesman of the day, a Minister who had built up his reputation by trading on the vices of men who were less cunning than he. Well did Vincent know that he was no match for such a diplomatist; but having once realized that the duty must be undertaken, he determined that there should be no flinching.

He went to Court in the old cassock in which he went about his daily work, and which was probably the only one he had. "You are not going to the palace in that cassock?" cried one of the Mission Priests in consternation.

"Why not?" replied Vincent quietly; "it is neither stained nor torn."

The answer was noteworthy, for a scrupulous cleanliness was characteristic of the man. As he passed through the long galleries of the Louvre he caught sight of his homely face and figure in one of the great mirrors that lined the walls. "A nice clodhopper you are!" he said amiably to his own reflection, and passed on, smiling.

Among the magnificently attired courtiers his shabby appearance created not a little merriment. "Admire the beautiful sash in which M. Vincent comes to Court," said Mazarin one day to the Queen, laying hold of the coarse woolen braid that did duty with poor country priests for the handsome silken sash worn by the prelates who

frequented the palace. Vincent only smiled—
these were not the things that abashed him; he
made no change in his attire.

At first it seemed as if his influence were to
be paramount in the Council. Nearly all the
priests of Paris had passed through his hands at
the ordination retreats and those who belonged
to the "Tuesday Conferences" were intimately
known to him. Who could be better fitted to
select those who were suitable for preferment?
Mazarin, it is true, objected to the Council on
principle, but that was simply because he considered that bishoprics and abbeys were useful
things to keep in reserve as bribes for his waver-
ing adherents. Certain reforms on which Vincent insisted were not to his mind either, although
he offered no opposition. It was not his way to
act openly, and he bided his time; the wonder
was that Vincent was able to do what he did so
thoroughly.

In the meantime it began to dawn upon the
public that the Superior of St. Lazare was for
the moment a man of influence. It was already
well known that he was a man of immense charity, with many institutions on his hands, several
of which were in urgent need of funds. It seemed
a very simple thing to offer him a large sum of
money for the poor on condition that he would
put in a good word for a brother or a nephew

who was just the man for a bishopric or anything else that might offer.

Vincent's reception of these proposals was dis-
concerting. "God forbid!" he would cry indig-
nantly. "Better that we should all go without the
barest necessaties of life."

Some would come with a recommendation from
the Queen herself, which made things doubly
embarrassing; but in spite of everything Vincent
remained faithful to his first determination—to
choose for bishoprics no priests save those worthy of the position by reason of their virtue and
learning.

Now, it was exceedingly unpleasant for needy
noblemen to be obliged to sue to a peasant priest
in a shabby cassock for the preferment of their
relations; but it became quite intolerable when
the shabby priest refused to listen.

"You are an old lunatic," said a young man
who had been refused a benefice through Vincent's agency.

"You are quite right," was the only answer,
accompanied by a good-natured smile.

Another day a gentleman who had come to
recommend his son for a bishopric was so angry
when Vincent explained that he did not see his
way to grant his request that he answered the
"impertinent peasant" with a blow. Vincent, without the slightest allusion to this treatment, qui-

etly escorted him downstairs and saw him into his carriage. Insulted another day in public by a magistrate whose interests he had refused to forward, the Superior of St. Lazare made the noble answer: "Sir, I am sure that you try to acquit yourself worthily in your office; you must allow me the same freedom of action in mine."

But Vincent's strangest adventure was with a Court lady of high rank, a certain Duchess in the household of the Queen. Catching her royal mistress in an unguarded moment, this lady succeeded in inducing the Queen to promise the bishopric of Poitiers to her son, a young man of very bad character. The Queen's courage, however, failed her at the prospect of breaking the news to M. Vincent, and she commissioned the Duchess to let him know of the appointment.

Off went the great lady to St. Lazare, and, flouncing into the Superior's presence, haughtily declared her errand. Vincent, aghast, begged her to sit down and talk the matter over, but Madame declined curtly. She was in a great hurry, she replied; the Queen had spoken; there was nothing more to be said. She would be obliged if he would make out the deed of nomination and take it to Her Majesty to sign.

What was to be done? To resist would only provoke; submission seemed the wisest, if not the only course.

Next morning at an early hour M. Vincent made his appearance at the palace with a roll of paper in his hand and was shown into the Queen's presence.

"Oh," said Her Majesty, not without some embarrassment, "you have brought me the nomination of the Bishop of Poitiers." Without a word, Vincent handed her the roll, which she proceeded to unfold.

"Why," she cried, "what is this? It is blank! The form is not drawn up at all!"

"If Your Majesty's mind is made up," said Vincent quietly, "I must beg you to write down your wishes yourself; it is a responsibility which my conscience forbids me to take." Then, noticing the hesitation of the Queen: "Madame," he said hotly, "this man whom you intend to make a bishop spends his life in public houses and is carried home drunk every night. That his family should want to get him out of Paris is not surprising, but I ask you if an episcopal see is a fitting retreat for such a person."

Convinced by Vincent's vehement presentation of the facts of the case, the Queen consented to revoke the nomination, but she openly confessed to him that she had not courage to face the Duchess. "Suppose you go and make my peace with her," she said pleasantly, despatching the unfortunate Vincent on this very disagreeable errand.

He was shown into the lady's presence and carried out his mission with the greatest possible tact, but the Duchess could not control her fury. Seizing a heavy stool, she flung it at the head of the unwelcome messenger, who bowed and retired from the house with the blood streaming from a wound in his forehead. The brother who had accompanied him and who was waiting in the antechamber, justly indignant, begged to be allowed to give the great lady a piece of his mind. "Come on," said Vincent; "our business lies in another direction." "Is it not strange," he said, smiling, a few moments later, as he tried to staunch the blood with his handkerchief, "to what lengths the affection of a mother for her son will go!"

Such incidents did not pass unnoticed by Mazarin, who looked with jealous eyes on Vincent's influence with the Queen. As time went on he resolved at any cost to rid the Court of the presence of this man, whose simple, straightforward conduct baffled the wily and defeated their plans; but an attempt to get him ejected from the Council met with such stormy opposition that the Prime Minister determined to change his tactics. There was no man whom he revered or admired so much as M. Vincent, he declared enthusiastically; no one who was of such use in the Council of Conscience.

But the summoning of the Council rested with Mazarin, and the intervals between its meetings became longer and longer. Anne of Austria's sudden spurt of energy—she was a thoroughly indolent woman by nature—began to die out as she became accustomed to her new responsibilities; she was only too glad to leave all matters of State to a man who declared that his only desire was to save her worry and trouble. In course of time the Council of Conscience ceased to meet, and the distribution of bishoprics and abbeys fell once more into the hands of Mazarin, who used them, as of old, for his own ends.

Vincent de Paul, in bitter grief and sorrow, was forced to witness an abuse that he had no longer any power to check. "I fear," he wrote in after years to a friend, "that this detestable barter of bishoprics will bring down the curse of God upon the country." A few years later, when civil war, pestilence and famine were devastating France, and Jansenism was going far to substitute despair for hope in the hearts of men, his words were remembered.

Chapter 9

THE JANSENISTS

WHILE Vincent de Paul was striving, by charity and patience, to renew all things in Christ, the Jansenists* were busy spreading their dangerous doctrines. When the Abbé de St. Cyran, the apostle of Jansenism in France, first came to Paris, Vincent, like many other holy men, was taken in by the apparent piety and austerity of his life. It was only when he knew him better, and when St. Cyran had begun to impart to him some of his ideas on grace and the authority of the Church, that Vincent realized on what dangerous ground he was standing.

"He said to me one day," wrote the Saint long afterwards to one of his Mission Priests, "that it was God's intention to destroy the Church as it is now, and that all who labor to uphold it

---

*So called from their founder, Cornelius Jansen, Bishop of Utrecht, who died, however, before his heresy had been condemned.

are working against His will; and when I told him that these were the statements made by heretics such as Calvin, he replied that Calvin had not been altogether in the wrong, but that he had not known how to make a good defense."

After such a statement as that there could be no longer question of friendship between Vincent and St. Cyran, although the latter, anxious not to break with a man who was held in such universal esteem as Vincent de Paul, tried to persuade him that he, St. Cyran, was really in the right, justifying himself in the elusive language which was more characteristic of the Jansenists than the frank declaration he had just made.

Vincent, however, was too honest and straightforward, too loyal a son of the Church, to be deceived. Realizing fully the danger of such opinions, he soon became one of the most vigorous opponents of the Jansenists, who, indeed, soon had cause to look upon Vincent as one of the most powerful of their enemies. But although he hated the heresy with all the strength of his upright soul, Vincent's charitable heart went out in pity to those who were infected with its taint, and it was with compassion rather than indignation that he would speak of St. Cyran and his adherents. Not until they had been definitely condemned by the Church did he cease his efforts to win them from their errors—efforts which were received, for the most part, in a spirit of vindictive bitterness.

The teaching of the Jansenists, like that of most other heretics, had begun by being fairly plausible. The necessity of reform among the clergy had come home to them forcibly, as it had to Vincent himself; the Jansenists' lives were austere and mortified. The book which contained their heretical doctrines, the Augustinus of Jansenius, was read by only a few, and these mostly scholars. That the Sacraments should be treated with the greatest respect and approached only by those who were fit to approach them seemed at first sight a very reverent and very proper maxim. Many people of holy lives took up this teaching enthusiastically, among them some of Vincent's own Mission Priests. When Antoine Arnauld, the youngest of the famous family which did so much to further Jansenism, published his book *Frequent Communion*, which might more truly have been called *"In*frequent Communion," it was received with delight and eagerly read. That Vincent clearly saw the danger is shown by one of his letters to a member of the Jansenist company who had written protesting against the attitude that St. Lazare was taking in the matter:

"Your last letter says that we have done wrong

in going against public opinion concerning the book *Frequent Communion* and the teaching of Jansenius. It is true that there are only too many who misuse this Divine Sacrament. I myself am the most guilty, and I beg you to pray that God may pardon me . . . . You say also that as Jansenius read all the works of St. Augustine ten times, and his treatises on grace thirty times, the Mission Priests cannot safely question his opinions. To which I reply that those who wish to establish new doctrines are always learned and always study deeply the authors of which they make use. But that does not prevent them from falling into error, and we shall have no excuse for sharing in their opinions in defiance of the censure of their doctrine."

The letter was answered by a second protest in favor of Arnauld's book, which was met by Vincent with equal energy:

"It may be, as you say," he writes, "that certain people in France and Italy have drawn benefit from the book; but for a hundred to whom it has been useful in teaching more reverence in approaching the Sacrament, ten thousand have been driven away . . . For my part, I tell you that if I paid the same attention to M. Arnauld's book as you do, I should give up both Mass and Communion from a sense of humility, and I should be in terror of the Sacrament, regarding it, in the spirit of the book, as a snare of Satan and as poison to the souls of those who receive it under the usual conditions approved by the Church. Moreover, if we confine ourselves only to what he says of the perfect disposition without which one should not go to Communion, is there anyone on earth who has such a high idea of his own virtue as to think himself worthy? Such an opinion seems to be held by M. Arnauld alone, who, having made the necessary conditions so difficult that St. Paul himself might have feared to approach, does not hesitate to tell us repeatedly that he says Mass daily."

It is evident that so cold and narrow a teaching could not but be repugnant to a man of Vincent's breadth and charity. The monstrous heresy held by the Jansenists that Christ did not die for all men, but for the favored few alone, filled him with a burning indignation. No one could have deplored more than he did the unworthy use of the Sacraments; but he held firmly to the truth that they had been instituted by a loving Saviour as man's greatest strength and as a protection against temptation and sin. And he was not going to believe that He who had been called the Friend of sinners and had eaten and drunk in their company would exact from men as a condition of approaching Him a perfection that they could never hope to attain without Him.

Indeed, the chief aim of the company of Mission Priests was to draw the people to the Sacraments as to the great source of grace, and it seemed to Vincent that the means taken by the Jansenists to destroy certain evils were very much more dangerous than the evils themselves. It was better, according to his opinion, even at the risk of abuse, to make the reconciliation of a sinner to his God too easy rather than too hard. The rule of the Mission Priests lays down that "one of the principal points of our Mission is to inspire others to receive the Sacraments of Penance and of the Eucharist frequently and worthily." The teaching of the Jansenists sought, on the contrary, to inspire such awe of the Sacraments that neither priests nor people would dare to approach them save at very rare intervals.

It was the great mass of the people—poor, simple and suffering, those children of God whom Vincent loved and in whose service the whole of his life had been spent—whose salvation was in danger. It was against them that the Jansenists were shutting the doors of salvation. Is it any wonder that Vincent de Paul fought against them as only men of strong conviction can fight, with heart and soul aglow in the battle? Compared with this all other evils were light.

His business was to relieve suffering, to comfort sorrow, but above all to help men to save their souls. There could be no yielding, no compromise with error.

Rightly, therefore, did the Jansenists see in Vincent de Paul the most dangerous of their enemies, and it was not surprising that both during his life and after his death they hated him and assailed him with abuse. He was "insincere, treacherous, a coward," they declared. They spoke of the "great betrayal"; they held him up to ridicule as an ignorant peasant; but Vincent went quietly on his way. The question "What will people say?" did not exist for him. He simply did his duty as it was made clear to him by God and his own conscience. It was hard to fight against such uncompromising honesty as his, and more than once the man whose ignorance the Jansenists had ridiculed tore their specious arguments to tatters with the weapon of his strong common sense.

Nevertheless, the dangers of Jansenism were a continual anxiety to Vincent, and there were other sorrows no less poignant to be borne. Foreign missions had been established in Africa and Madagascar, and in the latter station no less than twenty-seven Mission Priests had lost their lives. Some, it is true, had died the martyr's death; but the work had not prospered. It was difficult to get news from far countries in those days, and there were often such long intervals between the death of one priest and the arrival of another that any good that had been done was lost.

"There is nothing on earth that I desire so much as to go as your companion in the place of M. Gondrée," wrote Vincent to one who was just about to set forth on this dangerous mission; but the darker side of the picture is not left untouched. "You will need the strongest courage," he writes; "you will need faith as great as that of Abraham."

The Madagascar Mission was, humanly speaking, a failure; the natives were hostile, the missionaries not sufficiently numerous; it was necessary in the end to give up the enterprise.

The Lazarists were at work also in Poland, in Ireland, and in the Hebrides. Vincent had a gift for rousing zeal and charity in the hearts of others, and there were always plenty of volunteers for the most dangerous posts. But there were times when his heart nearly failed him at the news that came to him of the sufferings of some of his sons on their far-distant missions. There were times when apparent failure weighed him down with sorrow, and the death of young Mission Priests who had given their lives for the salvation of their fellowmen caused a grief almost too heavy to be borne. But Vincent knew

> How far high failure overtops the bounds
> Of low success.

He could afford to leave his work and theirs in
the hands of God. He had done what he could,
and God asks no more of any man.

Chapter 10

TROUBLES IN PARIS

ANNE of Austria had not been long Regent before it became apparent to everyone that the will of Mazarin lay behind all her actions. Mazarin, an Italian and an adventurer, was really at the head of affairs, said the people, and he was spending the public money in feasting and display while they were starving. That he was hated by the French is not surprising. Although famine was raging in several districts, and the country was greatly impoverished by war, the taxes were increased rather than diminished, and those who could not pay them were thrown into prison.

A few public men were found brave and honest enough to represent to the Queen the sufferings and wrongs of her people, but they might have saved themselves the trouble. The good resolutions that Anne of Austria had made at the beginning of her regency had long been forgotten. The question was referred, with all others, to Mazarin.

The Parliament at last took up the matter; men went about the streets of Paris shouting "Down with Mazarin!" A revolution was feared, and the Queen, with her young son, fled to St. Germain. The Royal troops in the meantime, under Condé, were blockading Paris; the rebellion known as the "Fronde" had begun.

Vincent de Paul was in a difficult position. His sympathies were wholly with the suffering people; but, although it had long ceased to meet, he was still a member of the Council of Conscience and owed allegiance to the Royal party.

What would become of the poor in Paris if the town were reduced to famine? This was the thought that was uppermost in his mind. On the other hand, he had always insisted that the Congregation of the Mission should in no way mix itself up with politics. The life of its members was to be a hidden life of prayer and labor for souls. The safest course was obviously to remain neutral and take no part in the matter; but his own safety was the last consideration likely to move him. Was it his duty to remain silent? That was the vital question. Could he do any good by speaking? Long and earnestly did he pray for guidance and, without a thought of the consequences to himself, decided at last to act.

Judging of others in the light of his own

straightforward honesty, it seemed to him that
if it were once clearly represented to the Queen
that it was Mazarin's presence alone that pre-
vented peace, she could not fail to see that it
was her duty to force him to withdraw. Surrounded as she was by courtiers who did not
dare to tell her the truth, she might be ignorant of how much she herself was to blame in
the matter. He had shamed her into doing what
was right in the matter of the Bishop of Poitiers.
Might he not succeed in awakening her conscience once more?

It was on his knees in the Church of St. Lazare
that Vincent resolved on the action that was at
best only a forlorn hope, but still worth trying.
With his usual prompt energy, the old man of
seventy-three mounted his horse and, accompanied only by his secretary, du Courneau, set out
for St. Germain. The Seine was in flood and
the water breast-deep on the bridge over which
they had to ride. Du Corneau avowed afterwards
that he was quaking with fright; but Vincent,
though wet to the skin, scarcely seemed to notice
that all was not as usual and rode on through
the floods in silence. Arrived at St. Germain, he
asked to see the Queen, who, thinking that he
had been sent by the people to make their peace
with her, admitted him at once to her presence.

With the straightforward simplicity that characterized all his dealings, he proceeded to state his errand. He had come, he said, to ask the Queen, for the sake of her country and her people, to rid herself of Mazarin and to forgive the rebels.

Anne of Austria listened in silence and gave no sign of either sympathy or displeasure. When the speaker had ended, she quietly referred him to Mazarin himself.

Vincent's hopes must have sunk low indeed at such a suggestion, but he was determined to go through with what he had begun. Confronted with the Cardinal, he earnestly represented to him that it was his duty to sacrifice himself for the good of the country; that his retirement would be an act of noble unselfishness which could not fail to win the blessing of Christ; that it would put an end to the sufferings under which France was groaning and save many innocent people from a fearful and horrible death. Mazarin had a sense of humor, and it was perhaps the only thing about him that responded to this appeal to his better feelings. It no doubt appeared to him sufficiently ludicrous that anyone should expect him to sacrifice himself for the sake of others, and probably those around him would have shared his opinion.

Yet Vincent was justified in his experiment. Long as had been his experience of the sin and

misery of men, it had not taught him, any more
than it did his Divine Master, to despair of
human nature. He had only employed his usual
methods with Mazarin: methods that had prevailed with so many souls. He had appealed to
the desire for good which he believed lay hidden in the heart of every man, no matter how
deeply it might be buried under the refuse of a
wasted life. He had appealed and failed—his
mission had borne no fruit, yet he could not
regret that he had undertaken it, although the
consequences were to be serious for himself. For
during his absence the fact that he had gone to
St. Germain had leaked out among the people,
and in one moment of anger all his claims on
their love and gratitude were forgotten.

"M. Vincent has betrayed us to the Queen!"
was the cry in the streets of Paris, while the
mob, falling on St. Lazare, pillaged it from top
to bottom, carrying off everything on which they
could lay hands. Vincent had gained nothing
and lost all; it was not even safe for him to
return to Paris, so great was the fury of the people; he had also won for himself the ill will of
both Mazarin and the Queen.

Yet with his usual humility and patience, he
blamed no one but himself. He had done, he
declared solemnly to du Courneau, that which
he would have wished to have done were he

lying on his deathbed; that he had failed was due solely and entirely to his own unworthiness.

And now, since it was better for every reason that he should not return to Paris, he determined to undertake a visitation of the Congregation of the Mission Priests and Sisters of Charity in every center where they were working in France. In spite of his weariness and his seventy-three years, he set forth on his journey, riding the old horse that was kept to carry him now that he could no longer travel on foot.

The suffering and misery that he witnessed, the horrors of famine and of war, only seemed to redouble his zeal to win the souls of men for their Maker. He knew the purifying force of suffering borne for God; he knew also the danger of despair. These poor creatures must be taught at any cost to lift their hearts to God, to bear their anguish patiently, to remember amid what agonies the Son of God had given His life for them. Wherever he went, his burning words and heroic example infused new life and courage into the hearts of his sons and daughters in Christ, who, in the life of abnegation they had undertaken, had often good reason for despondency.

Traveling in these lawless times was both difficult and dangerous, for the country roads were infested with robbers, but Vincent had no fear. He was seldom free from illness, which was sometimes increased by the privations he had to undergo, but he traveled on without resting.

Yet, amid all the new suffering which he had to witness and relieve, he was always mindful of his dear poor in Paris, which was still besieged by the troops of Condé. He had obtained a promise from the Queen during their last interview to let grain be taken into the town to feed the starving inhabitants, but she had not had sufficient energy to see that it was carried out.

The people were beginning to realize what they had lost in M. Vincent and to suspect that they had misjudged him. Hunger at last forced them to make terms with the Royal party, although the hated Mazarin was still supreme, and the Queen and her young son re-entered Paris in triumph.

But even Anne of Austria was not so foolish as to make her entry with the Cardinal at her side, and during the few weeks which still elapsed before he made his appearance in the capital, the Queen, free for a moment from the evil influence that stifled all her better impulses, wrote to Vincent, begging him to return. He was ill at Richelieu when the message reached him, and the Duchess d'Aiguillon, one of the most devoted of his Ladies of Charity, sent a little carriage to fetch him. She had known him long enough, however, to be sure that his love of mortification would prevent him from availing himself of what he would certainly look upon as a luxury. The carriage was accompanied by a letter from the Queen and the Archbishop of Paris ordering him in virtue of obedience to use it in the future for all his journeys. He obeyed, but sorely against the grain, and as long as he was obliged to avail himself of it always referred to the little carriage as his "disgrace."

"Come and see the son of a poor villager riding in a carriage," he would say to his friends when he took leave of them; and indeed, "M. Vincent's little carriage" soon became well known in Paris. It was always at the disposal of anyone who wanted it, and when Vincent used it himself it was generally shared by some of his beloved poor. The fact that it came in handy for taking cripples for a drive or the sick to the hospital was the only thing that reconciled him to its possession.

But the troubles of the Fronde were not yet at an end, and with Mazarin's return to Paris the discontent broke out afresh. The people were glad enough during the troublous times that followed to have Vincent once more in their midst.

Chapter 11

"CONFIDO"

WHEN at last peace was partially restored to the country, the number of poor people had enormously increased, and the charities that already existed were unable to cope with the misery and poverty in Paris. It was at this time that Vincent conceived the idea of founding a house of refuge for old men and women who had no means of gaining a livelihood. The foundation was placed in the charge of the Sisters of Charity. Work was provided for those who were able to do it; the proceeds went to keep up the establishment.

So successful was the venture and so happy were the poor creatures who found a comfortable home and kind treatment in their old age that the Ladies of Charity determined to found an institution on the same lines for all the beggars of Paris. A large piece of ground that had been used for the manufacture of saltpetre was accordingly obtained from the King, who also gave a large contribution of money toward the undertaking. The hospital, known as "La Salpêtrière" from the use to which the ground had formerly been put, was soon in course of building, but the beggars who were destined to fill it, many of whom were worthless vagabonds, showed very little desire for being shut up and employed in regular work. Vincent would have preferred to begin in a small way with those who were willing to come in; but the Ladies of Charity, in their enthusiasm, declared that it would be for the beggars' own good to bring them in by force, and the King was of their opinion. The Salpêtrière was soon crowded, while the sturdy rascals who infested the streets and begged under pretense of infirmity were suddenly cured at the prospect of leading a regular life and working for their living. Begging, at the risk of being taken off to the Salpêtrière, soon became an unpopular occupation, and the streets of Paris were a good deal safer in consequence.

In 1658, two years before his death, Vincent de Paul gave to the Congregation of Mission Priests its Rule and Constitutions. It was the work of God, he explained to them; there was nothing of his own in it. If there had been, he confessed humbly, it would only make him fearful lest his touch might spoil the rest. Those who listened to him and who had been witnesses of his long and holy life, his wisdom and his charity, knew better.

St. Lazare was a center where all fervent souls zealous for the service of God and the good of others met to find counsel and inspiration at the feet of its holy founder. Letters from all parts of the world and from all kinds of people in need of help and counsel kept the old man continually busy during the time he was not giving instructions, visiting the sick, or receiving those who came to ask his advice. He rose at four o'clock to the very end of his life and spent the first hours of the day in prayer, and this in spite of the fact that the last years of his life were years of acute bodily suffering.

His legs and feet, which for a long time had caused him great pain, became so swollen and inflamed that every step was torture. Ulcers, which opened and left gaping wounds, next made their appearance. It was said that in earlier years he had taken the place of an unfortunate man who had been condemned to the galleys and who was in consequence on the verge of despair, and that the malady from which he suffered had been caused by the heavy fetters with which his legs had been chained to the rowers' bench. It was several months, ran the tale, before his heroic action had been discovered and he was set at liberty, to bear for the rest of his life the penalty of his noble deed. When asked if this story were

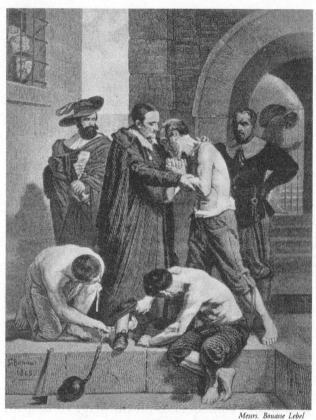

St. Vincent taking the place of the convict.

true, Vincent would change the subject as quickly as possible—which to those who knew how eagerly he always disclaimed, if he could, any action likely to bring honor to himself, seemed a convincing proof of its truth. With the greatest difficulty he was induced during the last years of his life to have a fire in his room and to use an extra coverlet, though he reproached himself bitterly in his last conferences to the Mission Priests and the Sisters of Charity "for this immortification."

But there were sufferings harder than those of the body. Mazarin was still in power; the "accursed barter of bishoprics" was still going on; and Vincent was forced to witness the very abuses against which he had fought so bravely during the brief time of his influence at Court.

The year 1660 brought two great sorrows: the death of M. Portail, the oldest and best beloved of Vincent's companions at St. Lazare, and that of Louise le Gras, the devoted Superior of the Sisters of Charity and the woman who would become known as St. Louise de Marillac. "You are going a little before me," he wrote to the latter when he heard that her life was despaired of, "but I shall meet you soon in Heaven." He was unable to go to her, for he could scarcely walk and was racked with fever. He would struggle on his crutches as far as the chapel to hear the Mass that he could no longer say and then go back again to his room, where he sat at a little table, working to the last, with a gentle smile of welcome for all who sought him.

The letters written during the last days of Vincent's life are full of the same good sense, the same lucid clearness of thought, the same sympathy and knowledge of the human heart that always characterized him. Two months before his death he gathered the Sisters of Charity together and gave them a conference on the saintly death of their Superior. With touching humility he asked his dear daughters to pardon him for all the faults by which he might have offended them, for any annoyance that his "want of polish" might have caused them, and he thanked them for their faithful cooperation in all his schemes of charity.

It was now such agony for him to walk to the chapel that his sons begged him to allow them to fit up a little oratory next to his room where Mass might be said, but Vincent would not hear of it. Then they implored him to allow himself to be carried in a chair, but, unwilling to give others the trouble of carrying him, he evaded the question until six weeks before his death, when he could no longer support himself on his crutches. During the nights of anguish, when his tortured limbs could find no rest on the hard straw mattress which he could never be prevailed upon to change for something softer, no complaint ever passed his lips. "My Saviour, my dear Saviour," was his only exclamation. On the days that followed these sleepless nights of pain, he was always smiling and serene. In spite of the weakness that oppressed him, he had help, advice and sympathy for everybody.

His reward was close at hand. On the 26th of September, 1660, having been carried to the chapel for Mass and Holy Communion, he was taken back to his room, where he fell asleep in his chair from sheer exhaustion, as he had so often done before. The brother who had charge of him, thinking that he slept longer and more heavily than usual, awakened him and spoke to him. Vincent smiled and answered, but instantly fell asleep again. The doctor was sent for, and roused him again. Once more the same bright smile lit up the old face; he answered, but had not sufficient strength to speak more than a few words. In the evening they gave him the Last Sacraments, and he passed the night in silent prayer. In the early morning one of the priests who belonged to the "Conferences," and who was making a retreat in the house, asked the dying man to bless all the priests for whom he had done so much and to pray that his spirit might be with them. "May God, who began the good work, bring it to perfection," was the humble answer.

A little later he was heard to murmur softly, "*Confido*"—"I trust"; and with these words on his lips, as a child puts its hand into that of his Father, he gently gave up his soul to God.

WORDS OF ST. VINCENT DE PAUL
(*Added by the Publisher, 1998.*)

The following are taken from The Voice of the Saints, *compiled by Francis W. Johnston, Burns & Oates, 1965; reprinted by TAN, 1986.*

Human nature grows tired of always doing the same thing, and it is God's will that this should be so because of the opportunity of practicing two great virtues. The first is perseverance, which will bring us to our goal. The other is steadfastness, which overcomes the difficulties along the way.

The more we conquer ourselves, the more He gives us of His grace; and if today we have had power to overcome one difficulty, tomorrow and the day after we shall be able to surmount others that are much greater and more distressing.

Feed upon the Will of God and drink the chalice of Jesus with your eyes shut, so that you may not see what is inside. Let it be enough for you to know that it is the cup of your sweet Jesus.

We must love our neighbor as being made in the image of God and as an object of His love.

Extend mercy toward others, so that there can be no one in need whom you meet without helping. For what hope is there for us if God should withdraw His Mercy from us?

We should strive to keep our hearts open to the sufferings and wretchedness of other people, and pray continually that God may grant us that spirit of compassion which is truly the spirit of God.

Tolerance is an important part of charity. Without it, it is difficult for two persons to get on together. Moreover, tolerance is the bond of all friendship, and unites people in heart and opinion and action, not only with each other, but in unity with Our Lord, so that they may really be at peace.

It is on humble souls that God pours down His fullest light and grace. He teaches them what scholars cannot learn, and mysteries that the wisest cannot solve He can make plain to them.

If we possessed every virtue, but lacked humility,

those virtues would be without root and would not last.

Be careful to give no credit to yourself for anything; if you do, you are stealing from God, to whom alone every good thing is due.

What was the life of Christ but a perpetual humiliation?

Let us not deceive ourselves. If we do not have humility, we have nothing.

We must remember that all incapacity and distress is sent to us by God. Life and death, health and sickness, are all ordered by Him; and in whatever form they come, it is always to help us and for our good.

There is great reason you should distrust yourself, but there is much greater reason that you should trust yourself entirely to your Divine Saviour.

When we have once placed ourselves entirely in the hands of God, we need fear no evil. If adversity comes, He knows how to turn it to our advantage, by means which will in time be made clear to us.

The following are taken from A Year With The Saints, *Anonymous, 1891; republished by TAN, 1988.*

Perfection consists in one thing alone, which is doing the will of God. For, according to Our Lord's words, it suffices for perfection to deny oneself, to take up the cross and to follow Him. Now, who denies himself and takes up his cross and follows Christ better than he who seeks not to do his own will, but always that of God? Behold, now, how little is needed to become a saint! Nothing more than to acquire the habit of willing, on every occasion, what God wills.

As it is most certain that the teaching of Christ cannot deceive, if we would walk securely we ought to attach ourselves to it with the greatest confidence and to profess openly that we live according to it, and not to the maxims of the world, which are all deceitful. This is the fundamental maxim of all Christian perfection.

The most powerful weapon to conquer the devil is humility. For, as he does not know at all how to employ it, neither does he know how to defend himself from it.

We ought always to consider others as our

superiors, and to yield to them, even though they be our inferiors, by offering them every kind of respect and service. Oh, what a beautiful thing it would be if it should please God to confirm us well in such a practice.

Our Lord says that whoever wishes to become greatest of all must make himself least of all. This is a truth that all Christians believe; how happens it, then, that so few practice it?

If we should well consider all that is human and imperfect in us, we should find but too much cause to humiliate ourselves before God and men, even before our inferiors.

The first step to be taken by one who wishes to follow Christ is, according to Our Lord's own words, that of renouncing himself—that is, his own senses, his own passions, his own will, his own judgment, and all the movements of nature, making to God a sacrifice of all these things, and of all their acts, which are surely sacrifices very acceptable to the Lord. And we must never grow weary of this; for if anyone having, so to speak, one foot in Heaven, should abandon this exercise, when the time should come for him to put the other there, he would run much the risk of being lost.

He who allows himself to be ruled or guided by the lower and animal part of his nature deserves to be called a beast rather than a man.

Whoever makes little account of exterior mortifications, alleging that the interior are more perfect, shows clearly that he is not mortified at all, either exteriorly or interiorly.

Mortification of the appetite is the A-B-C of the spiritual life.

Whoever cannot control himself in this will hardly be able to conquer temptations more difficult to subdue.

Whoever wishes to make progress in perfection should use particular diligence in not allowing himself to be led away by his passions, which destroy with one hand the spiritual edifice which is rising by the labors of the other. But to succeed well in this, resistance should be begun while the passions are yet weak; for after they are thoroughly rooted and grown up, there is scarcely any remedy.

We have never so much cause for consolation as when we find ourselves oppressed by sufferings and trials; for these make us like Christ

Our Lord, and this resemblance is the true mark of our predestination.

ABOUT THE AUTHOR

This book was authored by Mother Frances Alice Monica Forbes, a sister of the Society of the Sacred Heart, Scotland.

The future author was born on March 16, 1869 and was named Alice Forbes. Alice's mother died when she was a child, and her father became the dominant influence in her life, helping to form Alice's virile personality and great capacity for work. She was raised as a Presbyterian.

In 1900 Alice became a Catholic. The Real Presence in the Eucharist had been the big stumbling-block to her conversion, but one day she was hit by the literal truth of Our Lord's words: "This is My Body." Only a few months after her conversion, she entered the Society of the Sacred Heart, becoming a 31-year-old postulant. She seems to have received her vocation at her First Communion, when Our Lord kindled in her heart "the flame of an only love."

In the convent, Sister Forbes used her keen intelligence and strong will to make generously and completely the sacrifices that Our Lord asked of her each day. She put great store by the virtue of obedience. Much of the latter part of her life was spent in illness and suffering, yet she was always kind and uncomplaining—a charming person and a "gallant" soul. Throughout her sufferings the most important thing to her was the love of God. She died in 1936.

Mother Frances Alice Monica Forbes wrote many

books, including a series of interesting short lives of selected Saints called "Standard Bearers of the Faith." One of these books, that on Pope St. Pius X, was very highly regarded by Cardinal Merry del Val, who was a close friend of Pope Pius X.

Other works by Mother Frances Alice Monica Forbes include *St. Ignatius Loyola, St. John Bosco: Friend of Youth, St. Teresa, St. Columba, St. Monica, St. Athanasius, St. Catherine of Siena, St. Benedict, St. Hugh of Lincoln, The Gripfast Series of English Readers* and *The Gripfast Series of History Readers*, various plays, and a number of other books.

The above information is from the book *Mother F. A. Forbes: Religious of the Sacred Heart—Letters and Short Memoir*, by G. L. Sheil (London: The Catholic Book Club, 1948, by arrangement with Longmans, Green & Co., Ltd.).